THE
LAST OPIUM
DEN

BY THE SAME AUTHOR

Where Dead Voices Gather
The Nick Tosches Reader
The Devil and Sonny Liston
Chaldea
Trinities
Dino
Cut Numbers
Power on Earth
Unsung Heros of Rock 'n' Roll
Hellfire
Country

THE
LAST OPIUM
DEN

NICK TOSCHES

BLOOMSBURY

Published by Bloomsbury, New York and London
Distributed to the trade by Holtzbrinck Publishers

Library of Congress Cataloging-in-Publication Data

Tosches, Nick.
The last opium den / Nick Tosches.
p. cm.
ISBN 1-58234-227-X
1. Opium. 2. Tosches, Nick.--Journeys. I. Title.

HV581.T67 2000
362.293'3'092--dc21
[B]
2001043735

First published in *Vanity Fair* No. 481, September 2000
This edition published 2002

10 9 8 7 6 5 4 3 2 1

Typeset by Hewer Text Ltd, Edinburgh
Printed in Great Britain by Clays Limited, St Ives plc

Y OU SEE, I needed to go to hell. I was, you might say, homesick. But first, by way of explanation, the onion.

A friend of mine owns a restaurant that is considered to be one of the best Italian restaurants in New York. As is the case at most other Italian restaurants in Manhattan, the food is prepared by Dominicans or sundry other fellows of more exotic and indiscernible ethnic origin. This particular Third World truffle joint where I take my lunch possesses the added cachet of 'cucina toscana,' invoking the all-American theme park, Florence, where today one would be hard-pressed to find a vero fiorentino amid the overcrowding herd of estivating tourists that is Dante's revenge.

Anyway, there I sit, and I cannot help but see

and hear what surrounds me, as modish men raise glasses of wine and discuss balance, body, bouquet. My friend the proprietor is not a stupid man when it comes to business. He encourages them, engages them in the subtler points of their delusory expertise. The smile on his face – he has sold them for several hundred dollars what cost him far less – is to their purblind eyes both gratification and benediction, an acceptance of their expertise and knowing.

And I sit, and I sit, and I ponder the onion that has been placed before me. For this particular onion bespeaks more than the whole of the Uffizi the true nature of Italian creativity, more than the whole of Machiavelli the true nature of Tuscan cunning.

It is, to be precise, not even an onion, merely half an onion. Ah, but it is half a Walla Walla onion – this fact is flaunted – roasted and topped with a smidgen of caviar. The price is thirty-five dollars. As the cost of a single, one-pound Walla Walla onion is about a dollar, and the cost of beluga caviar well under twenty-five dollars an ounce, this half an onion and its smidgen must be worth about five or six bucks. Mysticized into a rare and precious delicacy by my friend, it is a very popular item: whenever the caviar runs out, the fifty-cent half-onion is served at a price of ten dollars.

As I ponder the onion, my memory wanders back, a quarter of a century ago and more, to this place before my friend took it over and made it into one of the great chi-chi joints of Manhattan. It was in those days a small semi-private eating establishment, a joint whose patrons were mostly gentlemen of a darkly taciturn sort. I can just imagine the gent by whose name the place was known setting before one of them half an American onion as if it were a treasure, and then suggesting not only that he pay for it but that he pay twenty-fold for it. It would have been the owner's end. For his truly were customers of worldly discernment. It is my friend's fortune that they are a dying breed, replaced by the neo-*cafoni* of today.

———

Anyway, let's get to what Kant called the ever elusive point. It has something to do with the halved onion, yes, but it has to do, too, with the balance, body, and bouquet of the wine.

Ours, increasingly, is the age of pseudo-connoisseurship, the means by which we seek fatuously to distinguish ourselves from the main of mediocrity. To sit around a bottle of rancid grape juice, speaking of delicate hints of black currant, oaken smoke, truffle, or whatever other dainty nonsense with which nature is fancied to have enlaced its taste, is to be a *cafone* of the first order. For if there is the delicate hint of anything to be sensed in any wine, it is likely that of pesticide and manure. Of a 1978 Château Margaux, one 'connoisseur' pronounces: 'With an hour's air, this wine unfolded to reveal scents of sweet cassis, chocolate, violets, tobacco, and sweet vanillin oak. With another ten years or so, this wine may evolve into the classic Margaux mélange of cassis, black truffles, violets, and vanilla.' As if this were not absurdity enough, there is 'a note of bell pepper lurking in the cassis.'

How could so sophisticated a nose fail to detect the cow shit with which this most celebrated estate in Bordeaux fertilizes its vines? A true wine connoisseur, if there were such a thing, would taste the pesticide and manure above all else: he would be not a *goûteur de vin* but rather a *goûteur de merde*. But there is no true connoisseurship of wine outside of those who know that the true soul of wine, *l'âme du vin*, is vinegar. It is in sipping straight those rare aged vinegars designated *da bere* that one truly tastes wonders: the real thing, an ichor far beyond the jive-juice of that industry of adjectives and pretense which was once the artless and noble drink of artless and noble peasants – peasants nobler and of greater connoissance than the moneyed suckers of today who have been conned into believing that the tasting of wine calls for words other than 'good,' 'bad,' or 'just shut up and drink.'

But, yes, the ever elusive point.

I'm sitting there, and I remember the old days, and I remember the taste of that vinegar, and I remember a thousand other things, and I remember the rarest taste of all: the taste of the breath of illimitableness.

Fuck this world of thirty-five-dollar onions and those who eat them. Fuck this world of pseudo-sophisticated rubes who could not recognize the finer things in life – from a shot of that vinegar to the first wisp of fall through a tree – let alone appreciate them, these rubes who turned New York into a PG-rated mall and who oh so loved it thus.

They were dead. The neighborhood was dead. The city was dead. Even the goddamn century was dead.

My limousine pulled up outside. It looked like a hearse. I decided to live. That is the ever elusive point: the point that eludes us all too often unto the grave.

⸻

I was born to smoke opium.

Don't get me wrong: I am against drugs, having long ago forsworn their use and embraced the spiritual path as set forth by *The Celestine Prophecy* and that guy with the big, shiny forehead. Drugs kill.

Nonetheless, I was born to smoke opium. More precisely, I was born to smoke opium in an opium den.

Why opium? Thomas De Quincey's description of it as 'the celestial drug' is not far from perfect: 'Here,' said he, 'was a panacea, a *φάρμᾰκον νηπενθές* for all human woes; here was the secret of happiness about which the philosophers had disputed for so many ages, at once discovered.' This celestial drug, this panacea, 'communicates serenity and equipoise to all the faculties, active or passive,' and 'introduces amongst them the most exquisite order, legislation, and harmony.' No one, 'having once tasted the divine luxuries of opium, will afterwards descend to the gross and mortal enjoyments of alcohol.'

Ponder these words; then pause to ponder too that De Quincey never experienced opium in its purest essence. As the title of his classic work, *The Confessions of an English Opium-Eater*, indicates, De Quincey never inhaled the vapors that are the transubstantiated soul of the drug in its most celestial form. De Quincey betrothed opium in London in the early years of the nineteenth century, before the pipe came west. He took his opium by means of the tincture known as laudanum, a dilution of the drug in alcohol, twenty-five drops of laudanum containing perhaps a single minuscule grain of opium. Thus the effects of the drug, no matter how celestial, were degraded and deadened by the overwhelming quantity of the 'gross and mortal' alcohol which constituted the basis of laudanum. The mixture of opium with wine is alluded to in the *Odyssey*, and as Homer praises it mightily and knowingly, we can assume that the first and greatest among poets was no stranger to the celestial drug.

Both as medicine and as holy panacea, opium is older than any known god. Its origins lie in the prehistoric mists of the early Neolithic period. It was glorified in Mesopotamia and in Egypt, emerged in the Mediterranean region with the primal Great Mother, and remained tied to her, in her evolving guises, through the archaic and classical periods. As attested by Homer, it was a theophanous substance to the Greeks, who gave the wondrous poppy-sap its name, ὄπιον, Latinized as opium. The Doric word for the opium poppy, μάκων, which to the classical Greeks became μήκων – mekōn – gave the opium-rich town of Kyllene its olden name of Mekone, or Poppytown. There, in a sanctuary of Aphrodite, a gold-and-ivory image of the goddess later stood, an apple in one hand, a poppy in the other.

As with the mysterious confluences of religion,

there are echoes and enlaced winds, defying both history and linguistics, that pervade the mysterious world of opium. Throughout Asia, regardless of language or of dialect, the many words for opium are resonant of the oldest known word for it, which itself is a resonance of the unknown. From the Poppytown of ancient Greece to the ancient town in the opium heartland of modern Turkey whose name, Afyan, and the name of opium are one; from vanished Mekone to the Mekong river that today runs through the Golden Triangle: it is as if the stuff, transcending time and place, imbued all voice with its strange numinous breath.

De Quincey never smoked opium. Had he done so, one can only imagine the extent to which his extravagant reverence would have been drawn. But as the origins of the holy marriage between man and opium are lost to the mists of the primordium, so too are those of the Big Smoke. There is the tale, commonly accepted as truth, that the Dutch introduced the practice of smoking opium in a tobacco pipe to the Chinese at the turn of the eighteenth century. But it is impossible to 'smoke' opium in a tobacco pipe, as opium neither burns nor converts into smoke. Rather, it is distilled into vapor through a chemistry quite unlike that of any other 'smoking.' The process, or art, of this chemistry, though quite simple when mastered, demands many things: the combined exactitudes of appropriate lamp oil, design of lamp and lamp chimney, properly trimmed wick of fitting fiber; the craft of employing the slender spindle to heat, spin, and knead the opium – to say nothing of the lengthy previous preparations of the opium – prior to its insertion into the tiny hole of the pipe bowl, or damper; the precisely manipulated distance and downward angle of the pipe bowl over the lamp flame. These are all necessary to facilitate the exact degree of latent heat required to convert the opium into vapor. There are those who might say that the chemistry of opium smoking is chemistry as much in the original sense of the word – *chymistrie:* the dark and magic art of alchemy – as in the current.

It has been put forth that opium smoking was practiced in China as early as 1500, that the stuff itself had been introduced to China by Arab traders as early as the year 400. Recent archaeological discoveries in Cyprus have brought to light what very well may be opium pipes dating to the late Bronze Age – discoveries detailed in the deep-seeking scholarship of Mark David Merlin's *On the Trail of the Ancient Opium Poppy*. How was the secret of the Big Smoke – the key to paradise – lost for almost 2,000 years, if the practice was indeed known to Bronze Age Cyprus? The mystery befits the mystery of its powers.

All that is known for certain is that opium smoking was widespread in China by the mid-18th century, and that its vapors reached Europe and America a hundred years later, about the time of poor De Quincey's death in the country that had started it all by imposing its

Indian opium on China. But this is no place to touch upon the Opium Wars, nor upon the fact that nothing really began either with Europe's bringing from India to China what Alexander the Great had brought to India, or even with that Bronze Age pipe so long ago. When God put His mouth to the nostrils of Adam, there was probably opium on His breath.

—

The one irrefutable fact is there is nothing like opium on the face of this earth. For more than 5,000 years, from 'the plant of joy,' as the Sumerians knew it, to 'the celestial drug' of De Quincey's seduction and thralldom, 'the forbidden, fabulous opium' (in the words of another addict, Jean Cocteau) has been the dangerous glimpse of paradise from which no initiate has passed unchanged. This, the supernal power of opium, is not a fact of ancient mysteries and visionary poets alone. As acknowledged by Edward M. Brecher, whose monumental study *Licit and Illicit Drugs* was in 1989 recognized as a 'towering work' by the straitlaced *New York Times*, the nineteenth-century medical community commonly described opium in terms as mighty with awe as those of any Mesopotamian seer: 'God's own medicine.'

So, then. Why opium? That's why. And why the opium den? The answer to that can be expressed in one word: romance.

Visions of dark, brocade-curtained, velvet-cushioned places of luxurious decadence, filled with the mingled smoke and scents of burning joss sticks and the celestial, forbidden, fabulous stuff itself. Wordless, kowtowing servants. Timelessness. Sanctuary. Lovely loosened limbs draped from the high-slit cheongsams of recumbent exotic concubines of sweet intoxication. Dreams within dreams. Romance.

Yes, I was born to smoke opium, born to smoke it in an opium den. There were a couple of problems, however. For one thing, opium is illegal. True, I am no saint, but I am no scofflaw either.

I suffer from diabetes. My failure to maintain control of this disease through diet, exercise, medication, and the avoidance of stress has mystified physicians, including the foremost of endocrinologists. Only recently was it brought to my attention that, among its many proven age-old medicinal uses – as a cure for dysentery, asthma, rheumatism, etc. – opium was considered to be effective in the treatment of diabetes.

The thought of breaking the law troubled me gravely. But I have always had another disease as well: the desire to live. To not do everything in my power to save my own life would be to break the law of God and of the sanctity of life as well. I deliberated. I meditated. I prayed. I shared my thoughts with a priest – I did not share with him the bit about the envisioned gams draped from the slits of the doped-up broads' dresses; there was no need to – and he told me, Go for it. I felt better. Now if ever I ran afoul of the law, I could blame it on the priest.

–

But, as I said, there were a couple of problems. Now that this law-abiding diabetic was right with God, he faced the second of those problems. It was almost impossible to get opium these days anywhere in America or Europe. For two years, with the help of many, even those not unfamiliar with the less savory strata of society, I searched. New York, nothing. Paris, nothing. London, nothing. Rome, nothing. Berlin, nothing. Finally, from a Turkish art dealer, I got hold of something that was supposed to be opium. It looked and felt like all the other stuff that was bought and sold as opium years ago when it was not so rare. God only knows what this stuff was, what it had always been: some sort of Turkish junk, perhaps containing something of opium, more likely something of the toxic residue of opium; but it wasn't opium, and, as I was to discover, it never had been. Besides, even if it was, even if it ever had been, no one had a real opium pipe, no one knew how to use one. Sure, one could eat it, stick it up one's ass, 'smoke' it in a hash pipe, but whatever effect it had, other than to make one ill, was all in the suggestibility of one's mind.

As for opium dens, forget it.

America had been involved in the opium trade since the early nineteenth century, when John Jacob Astor, among others, made a fortune smuggling tons of Turkish opium to Canton. And as laudanum, opium was no less familiar in the States than it was in England. But it was the Chinese immigrants, come to build the railroads and work the mines, who brought the paradise of the pipe to America.

The phrase 'opium den' had barely entered the language when San Francisco banned the smoking of opium within its city limits in the 1870s. For thirty years and more, as the Chinese population spread across America, an ever in- creasing number of opium dens, amid ever increasing anti-opium legislation, operated in open secrecy in every major city. The fever of public indignation grew as the habitués of the dens became ever less confined to the Chinese whose souls were as nought on the scales of American values. Periodicals and their readers thrived on lurid exposés, vicarious visits often embellished by fancy, or wrought of fancy pure, to those lairs of iniquity where gangsters, the demimonde, and the slumming vampires of Broadway and high society – in short, the hip – gathered together in the languor of the irredeemable.

The word 'hip,' whose currency was common enough for it to have appeared in print by 1904 – around the time, coincidentally, that the first opium song, 'Willie the Weeper,' seems to have originated – may have derived from the classic, age-old, pelvic-centered, side-lying opium-smoking position, and may have been used originally as a sign of mutual recognition and reference by those who were in the know about the big sweet smoke.

Amid raids, seizures, and arrests, opium dens continued to operate in New York and elsewhere. In the early decades of the twentieth century, as the drug trade was taken over by the Judeo-Christian coalition that came to control crime, Jewish and Italian names became almost as common as Chinese names in the reports of those arrested for smuggling, selling, and den-running. While the old Chinese opium smokers died off, the new drug lords actively cultivated a market for the opium derivatives, first morphine and then heroin, two nineteenth-century inventions that offered far greater profit margins – the Onion Principium – than opium itself.

These drugs offered oblivion, not ethereality, a rush into the void rather than a slow drifting to blissful serenity. Younger people – strangers more and more to opium smoking as its presence ebbed, or knowing it only in the increasingly impure form in which the Judeo-Christian consortium delivered it forth; strangers more and more perhaps to the possibility of serenity itself, or to the appeal of any slow drifting – were easily won over to oblivion and the visceral rush. They did not want a drawn-out ceremony, a ritual; they wanted the rush. While the cultivation and supply of opium increased beyond knowing, the smoking of opium vanished. Its end was an ouroboros: a decrease in demand, with no cause to rekindle or sustain that fading demand, as those who were the satisfiers of demand could make far more money by processing opium into heroin. The flower of joy, crushed into the flower of misery, could yield tenfold in gold, tenfold in addiction, and thus, exponentially, on and on.

By the late 1930s, opium dens were rare. A 1936 book, *Chinatown Inside Out*, tells of fake opium dens operated in cahoots with tourist-bus companies to offer a bit of 'false local color.' (As for false local color, the book's author, Leong Gor Yun, was in reality the multi-pseu-donymous Virginia Howell Ellison, the author of *The Pooh Cook Book of 1969* and *The Pooh Party Book of 1971*.)

The bust, in the fall of 1950, of a den in

St. Paul, Minnesota, seemed a beguiling anachronism.

The last known opium den in New York was a second-floor tenement apartment at 295 Broome Street, between Forsyth and Eldridge Streets, at the northeastern edge of Chinatown. It was run by the apartment's tenant, a Chinese immigrant named Lau, who was fifty-seven when the joint got raided and his ass got hauled away. There were a few old pipes and lamps, ten ounces of opium. And forty ounces of heroin. The date was June 28, 1957. That was it. The end of the final relic of a bygone day.

I was assured by friends and contacts around the world that the same ouroboros had wound through every continent. Even in Asia, I was told, the opium dens had vanished within the last twenty years. It was the same story, even in the most corrupt and lawless of lands: the old smokers had died off, the kids wanted the rush, the drug lords wanted to keep it that way. Old and young who had lived their lives in these places, old and young who had looked upon and skulked through this world as had Sir Richard Burton. Sinners and saints, lawmen and criminals, drug addicts and scholars, lunatics and seekers. They all told me the same: there ain't no such thing no more; them days are gone.

But I could not believe it. I would not believe it.

—

I remember Hong Kong. I was here long ago. I did not then know from vinegar, other than the kind you mixed with oil; let alone did I know from opium. Hong Kong then was a city where you could get whatever you wanted, whenever you wanted it. There was no night, no day: only the light of the sun and the light of neon, and the lush darkness, the endless rushing midnight, the true soul of the place, that imbued even the blazing dawn, where sun and neon became for one still instant the electric haze that was the single heartbeat of rest – taken upright at a bar or a gambling table, or abed in luxuriance of silk and faintly perfumed breath – that preceded the waking fiery breath of a dragon and a city that were one.

This is what I remember as I roam through Hong Kong these many years later, in the wake of the region's return to Chinese sovereignty. It was rightfully so that the Nobel laureate Milton Friedman, America's greatest economist, praised Hong Kong as the exemplar of free-market capitalism, the only true capitalist city on earth. The fierceness of that freedom was the fire in the breath and the neon in the blood of the dragon. Now the fire is but smoke and ember, the neon anemic, the dragon feeble and more of shadow than of substance. Communism is a cement mixer that spews forth drab and indistinguishable gray concrete. Wherever Communism comes, everything – the physical architecture of the place, then its soul – turns drab and gray, and in its weakness crumbles to a drabness and a grayness uglier and grimmer by far.

―

Leaving my hotel, I walk out into the night, across Salisbury Road, to the wide neon boulevard of Nathan Road, whose countless winding side streets and intertwining alleys were the places where all could be had for a price, be it sex or murder, a drink of rarest snake blood or a shot of purest dope, gambling or guns, gold or embroidery or jade, amulets to ward off demons or to court their favor.

The Chinese food here is still the best in the world. My friend, a gentleman more advanced in years and in dignity than myself, is a man of respect who has lived in Hong Kong all his life and knows its labyrinthine streets and alleys like the veins on the back of his hand. (I here pause, after deleting the good Chinese name that followed the phrase 'my friend' in the above sentence. I pause to state the obvious, as I have been instructed by legal counsel that 'it is necessary to mention that names have been changed,' as indeed they have been. In some cases, as in the above instance, I have disposed of names entirely. Now back to 'my friend.') He takes me where I want to go, to the restaurants where no English is spoken and where white men are not welcome, the restaurants where, in his presence and with his benison, I eat like an emperor, or at least like someone who knows what he's doing.

Handfuls of scurrying shrimp, their tiny eyes bright and their soft shells lovely with the delicate translucent blue of life, are scooped from a seawater tank, presented to us on a platter kicking and scrambling, their leaping escape to the carpet prevented only by the expert maneuvers of the waiter, who then dispatches them rapidly into a black castiron wok sizzling over high fire at tableside, douses them with strong fermented-rice liquor – to make them drunk in their dying, and thus supple of flesh – sets the liquor aflame, and even more expertly maneuvers their containment during the intensified frenzy of their fast death by fire.

Succulence and death. Cabbage, pig tripe, and white radish. Cobra soup – the more venomous the serpent, the more potent the tonic; gelatinous and steaming and delicious beyond description – garnished with petals of snow-white chrysanthemum. Later, amid the crowded stalls of the night market, we watch as an elderly Chinese man hands over a small fortune in cash to another elderly man, a snake seller much esteemed for the rarity and richness of poison of his stock. The snake man pockets the money, narrows his eyes, and with a studied suddenness withdraws a long, writhing serpent from a cage of bamboo. Holding it high, his grasp directly below its inflated venom glands, its mouth open, its fangs extended, he slashes it with a razor-sharp knife from gullet to midsection, the movement of the blade in his hand following with precise rapidity the velocity of the creature's powerful whiplashings, which send its gushing blood splattering wildly. Laying down the blade, the snake man reaches his blood-drenched hand with medical exactitude into the open serpent, withdraws its still-living bladder, drops it into the eager hands of his customer, who, with gore dripping from between his fingers onto his shirt, raises the pulsing bloody organ to his open mouth, gulps it down, and wipes and licks away the blood that runs down his chin.

'Arthritis,' my friend observes to me by way of explanation. 'Good live bladder. Top dollar.'

This – what we have witnessed here in the Hong Kong night – is true connoisseurship, pure of any note of bell pepper lurking in the cassis. It is the same, true connoisseurship that surrounds the secret brewing techniques of the best snake soups, the pickling techniques and proper extraction, morseling, and savoring of delicacies such as pig-face.

Surely, I figure, if this sort of rare and fine connoisseurship lingers furtively on, there must yet exist somewhere amid the labyrinths of this vast city at least one last sanctum of that greatest of connoisseurships.

Hua-yan jian, they were called: flower-smoke rooms. The flowers were courtesans; the smoke was opium. The flower-smoke room: the celestial perfumed salon of timeless serenity where one could suck on paradise while being paradisiacally sucked.

The flower-smoke rooms, which thrived in Shanghai and Hong Kong from the ninteenth century until the early 1930s, were of all sorts, from lowly brothels to chambered quarters of sybaritic splendor. The vast majority of them, I have been assured, were of the former sort.

My friend told me that the last and lowliest of the *hua-yan jian* had shut down many years ago. As for even the most low-down, humblest, and flowerless hole-in-the-wall remnant of an opium den, there was not one left in all of Hong Kong. Now, under Chinese rule, it would be almost impossible to find opium, let alone a place where it could be properly smoked. Even in the new Shanghai, where child prostitution has burgeoned amid the tourist attractions, not a flower-smoke room is to be found.

———

My friend was not alone in telling me this. An acquaintance close to sources in local law enforcement, after inquiries among those sources, conducted secretly on my behalf and with fine wile, was told that, while drugs were still common, the presence of opium in Hong Kong was practically nil. There was still opium to be found in the boomtowns of neighboring Guangdong Province. There, in Guangzhou, the sale of opium is punishable by death. There, in Shenzhen, a few days before I was in Hong Kong, eleven drug dealers, including a teenage girl, were taken directly from trial to execution.

I stand while toward midnight under the big whorish neon lips outside the Red Lips Bar on Peking Road. It is like standing in church light, filtered softly through dark stained glass: a comforting, a respite, a connection with old ways, old values, and sleaze gone by.

In a music shop, I buy a couple of CDs by one of the most revered of Hong Kong's elder entertainers, the singer of Cantonese opera who was known as Sun Ma Sze Tsang, among other stage names, and whose real name was Tang Wing Cheung. He was born in Guangdong Province in 1916, and he died in Hong Kong in 1997, a few months before the return to Chinese rule. Half a century ago and more, licenses to smoke opium were issued to certain inveterate smokers of means and standing. I do not buy the CDs because I like Cantonese opera or the singer known as Sun Ma Sze Tsang. I buy them because he is said to have been the last of the licensed opium smokers. With his death, at the age of eighty-one, on April 21, 1997, the legal smoking of opium, long unique unto him, came to its end.

I turn to yet another native acquaintance, a gentleman of a different sort, with whom I am able to penetrate the inner circles of the triads of the Sham Shui Po district, an area so dark that its reputation as a black market serves as a veneer of relative respectability.

There are several meetings with different men, different groups of men. Again and again, the hushed word for opium, *ya-p'iàn*.

In the end, there is nothing that the night stalkers and gangs of Sham Shui Po cannot get for me. Perhaps a kilo of pure No. 4 heroin? A ton of pure No. 4 heroin? A truckload of pills? Artillery or explosives? American hundred-dollar bills complete with watermark, safety thread, and intaglio as fine as that of the Bureau of Engraving and Printing? Or perhaps I should like to buy – we're talking outright ownership here – a few women, children, whatever. No problem.

But no one can bring me to an opium den. Why? Because there is no such thing.

I lean inside the hotel elevator. My tired eyes settle on a stylish framed placard advertising the Club Shanghai on the mezzanine level: SCANDAL AND DECADENCE – 1930s STYLE. Downstairs, at breakfast, I read in the *Hong Kong Standard* of the government's attempts 'to woo a Disney theme park to Hong Kong.'

I walk into a joint on Patpong Road in Bang-kok, sit down on a banquette near the bar, and within a minute there is one naked scrawny girl to my left, another to my right, a third crouched between my legs beneath the little table set before me. The brace that flanks me have squirmed and curled their way under my arms, drawn each of my hands to a breast; the one under the table strokes my crotch and thighs with her fingers and head. On the raised stage in the center of the room, five more girls perform simultaneously, one at each corner, one in the middle: two squat to lift Coke bottles with their pudenda, two undulate with spread legs against stage poles, one lies with a leg raised high, masturbating and wagging her tongue. With one hand, I squeeze a nearby nipple between thumb and forefinger. She whose nipple it is responds instantaneously with a swooning moan so overdone that when I laugh she just as instantaneously bursts into laughter herself. The three of them will continue to work me either until I agree to take one or two or all of them upstairs, or anywhere I please – 150 baht, the equivalent of about four American dollars, to the house; another few hundred baht per girl, negotiated separately with them, for the night – or until I slap them away in anger like flies. This is why most Westerners come to Bangkok.

'They like Americans,' says an expatriate friend who has long been involved with one of the loveliest of the countless girls who work the joints of Patpong Road and the Nana district. 'The British are cheap, the Japanese want to put out cigarettes on them, and the Germans are, well, German.'

Most of the girls are Isaan, he tells me, from the northeast of Thailand, where an insectivorous cuisine is common. We sit in the warm night air of a small cloistered square – more of a courtyard – in the heart of Nana, near where his girlfriend lives and works. The girls here are much more sedate, cooler, less rabid than those of Patpong Road.

Between two bars, directly opposite a joint proclaiming, TOP FLOOR 250 GIRLS, is a little Buddhist shrine strewn with the flowers of the girls' frequent offering. The passage from the courtyard leads to the main drag of Sukhumvit Soi 4, where, amid much smoke of oil and grill, street vendors cater to the taste of the girls: fried grasshoppers, fried grubs of different size and kind, fried beetles, served forth hot from bubbling oil in parcels of white greasy paper; roast-blackened baby sparrows, roast-blackened chicken feet, straight from the grill on skewers of splinter wood. My buddy has brought us a package of fried grasshoppers to share at the outdoor bar where we sit. The girls pay ten baht, the equivalent of about twenty-five cents, for these scavenged or foraged delectables; everybody else pays twice that.

'Have you ever had the maggots?' I ask, as he chews a mouthful of the almost tasteless fried grasshoppers, a fitting bar food, all salt and crunch, but a good source of protein as well. He shakes his head.

'It's the baby birds that scare me,' I say.

Girls pass, approach the shrine, sweep back their hair with both hands in ritual obeisance.

'They ask for a good night, a customer who treats them kindly,' observes my friend.

Under the third precept of Buddhism, which demands abstinence from all sexual misconduct, twenty groups of women are listed as forbidden. Whores are not included among them.

Again, flowers without smoke. My expatriate friend has been living in Bangkok for many years, and he tells me that he has never heard of the existence of an opium den.

And yet Bangkok, with its vast Chinatown, is said to have boasted the biggest opium den in the world, an immense establishment on New Road, the oldest paved street in Bangkok. This biggest of opium dens is said to have been able to accommodate 8,000 smokers at once, and to have maintained a stock of 10,000 pipes. It is said to have operated into the early 1960s.

Bored with the tourist joints of Patpong Road and Nana, I have asked another friend, a Bangkok native whose good name I shall leave unsullied, to take me where the Thai guys go. We drive across town to what he says is the best eating place in Bangkok. It is a nameless operation in a nameless alley near Songsawad Road in Chinatown. It does not exist by day, when the alley is crowded with trucks and the dense traffic of human haulers. It exists for only three hours, between six and nine at night, when a few old, unsteady folding tables and folding chairs are set out in the alley near the foodstuffs, fires, pots, and pans of two suddenly materialized cooking stalls. At the stroke of six, BMWs and chauffeured Mercedes-Benzes pull up at the corner of the alley; in minutes, all the chairs are taken. There are no menus. Some nights there are napkins, some nights not. Tonight is a lucky night.

There are five tones in spoken Thai, each lending different meaning to a similar sound. I have no idea what is being said between my friend and the stall tenders, but some minutes later there arrive bowls of steaming fish-ball and noodle soup. The most coveted bird's nests for the most precious of Chinese bird's-nest soups are Thai: the swiftlet nests gathered from amid the paintings on the walls of a cave in the high, sheer cliffs of Koh Phi Phi Leh, an uninhabited island off the southern coast of the peninsula. A bowl of soup made from one of these small nests can cost the equivalent of between two hundred and three hundred dollars. And yet its taste is as nothing compared with the taste of the soup in this nameless dark alley. Its price is sixty baht, the equivalent of a dollar and change.

Throughout the night's roamings, my friend explains that opium is a dead drug. The drug of

Thailand today, as throughout Southeast Asia, is *ya ba*, 'crazy medicine' – speed. While Thailand has all but eradicated the opium poppy in its effort to ingratiate itself with the Western powers, the country is still a central transport area for the heroin refined from the opium of the poppy fields of other, nearby regions. More and more, however, the transport caravans of the drug lords are hauling truckloads of amphetamine as well as of heroin.

As my friend saw and convincingly expressed it, the relatively recent and fast-growing spread of cheap and plentiful *ya ba* is a plague that will ultimately prove far more destructive than heroin to the foundations of Asian society, just as speed itself is, in the long run, far more physically destructive and deadly a drug than heroin. I could go to the drug bazaars of the slums of Klong Toey, west of Bangkok. There I could buy all the marijuana, all the crack, all the heroin, all the speed that any man could ever crave. But I would find no opium.

In the morning, I meet with an older friend of my friend. He remembers the opium-den days of Bangkok, and he knows Chinatown well. He takes me to an ancient 'teahouse' of many stories on Yaowarat Road in Chinatown. At the second landing, he exchanges words with a group of ominous-looking men gathered round a circular table. One of them nods, and we proceed through a curtain into a narrow hall that becomes a maze of narrow halls, lined with small rooms. An old woman takes us to one of the rooms, brings us two small, dirty teacups and a pot of hot tea. A teenage girl enters, then another. These girls bear numbers, pinned to their open shirts. One is No. 58. The other, astoundingly, is No. 199. How many girls does this maze hold? I like No. 58, and, ahem, she says she likes me. She pours tea into the dirty cups, begins stroking my crotch. She looks fresh, new to this place and still full of life. She speaks a little English, and while my companion lies back to enjoy his tea, I employ the only Thai that I have almost learned to properly intone: *fin*, which, in the second of its five tones, means opium. She mistakes my meaning as a desire for heroin. She seems shocked, makes gestures of jabbing a spike into her slender forearm. 'Why want? No good.' Then blasé: 'We buy, then we make love.' My companion explicates in Thai. She seems no longer shocked but, rather, nonplussed, regarding me with a bemused smile as if I were a most odd man, misplaced in time.

On the way out, my companion speaks again with men round the table. Yes, this place, with its maze of rooms, had once been an opium den. But that was long ago. 'Many year, no *fin*,' the eldest of them says to me.

After days and nights in Chinatown, days and nights of wandering and searching pleasure palaces and hellholes of Bangkok, I begin to see that the true presiding god of this place is Colonel Sanders. Images of the Colonel are everywhere; franchises abound, many of their entrances graced with life-size white plaster statues of the Giver of Fowl.

More than two hundred Kentucky Fried Chicken franchises in Thailand, not a single opium den. Somebody tells me that I should not leave Bangkok without trying the really special coffee at this really cool new place called Starbucks.

—

By land, by water, by plane. Across this river, through that jungle, each town dustier than the last.

Phnom Penh. I've been practicing my Cambodian for days, a vocabulary of one word whose proper pronunciation lies vaguely between *a pian* and *a phian*. Not far from the hotel where I'm staying, there's a small, enclosed plaza that is notorious for its murder rate: a killing or so every week. At one corner of the plaza is a very big barroom, made all the bigger by the absence of a wall and part of the roof, which appear to have been lost to an explosion some years ago, thus opening the place to the limitless black Cambodian night. The bar, its entrance guarded by a machine-gun-bearing sentry, is loud with harsh Asian rock 'n' roll and screaming of all sorts. Outside, a bit beyond where the missing wall used to be, is a gigantic screen on which is projected a Malaysian monster movie with Cambodian subtitles, and the soundtrack screams that accompany every drive-in-size out-of-focus bloodletting occasionally drown out the screams of the place. In an area near the front of the bar, a large and formidable Cambodian woman, perhaps in her late fifties, stalks amid a gaggle of young girls, toward whom she directs not infrequent screams of her own. When our eyes meet, her face of stone turns to a vicious smile that flashes gold teeth, and she draws near.

'What you want, I have. All Phnom Penh. Anything. I have. You say me what want. I have.'

'*A pian*. You have *a pian*?'

She nods sternly, arrogantly, happily. 'Yes. I

have. What you want, I have. You say me what kind. I have all. Have fifteen-year-old. Have thirteen-year-old, have twelve-year-old. What you want?'

Aged opium?

'Here, look this.' She snaps a snarl of clipped consonants, and a very small, very young, tawny-skinned girl joins us. 'Here no many years. Like new. Twelve year. Not even bleed. See' – she flicks the girl's lowered head upward – 'like baby.' I can't tell if the girl is actually adolescent or older and stunted by malnutrition. She is very skeletal. Her shoulder blades are sharp.

On the upstairs open-air porch of the Foreign Correspondents' Club, the lazy meandering of a lizard on a post near my table, the nighttime breeze from the Tonle Sap River, and the good, familiar taste of a hamburger are like a calmative. I hook up with a guy who knows his way around. He hooks me up with a Cambodian guy who really knows his way around and who will do anything for money.

Through the swarm of beggars outside the club, the Cambodian guy leads me about a mile or so along Sisowath Quay, then down a dark backstreet, to a scrap-patched bamboo shack. There is a group of shirtless, scrawny Cambodian men. There is a long, involved discussion, with no small amount of obvious debate among the group of shirtless, scrawny men. My companion explains to me that the legacy of the Khmer Rouge is that Cambodian no longer trusts Cambodian. In the end, there is assent among the men. They will sell me opium pellets for eating. But I don't want to eat opium. I want to smoke opium. I want to smoke opium in an opium den. There is no opium den, they say. They do not even have a pipe. They know of no one who has a pipe. We leave.

My companion assures me that out in the wild swamp country where the Tonle Sap and the Bassac and the Mekong are one, there are men who still smoke opium. One of them is a friend of his. This friend is beyond the reach of any telephone. All we can do is go to the swamp country and hope that we will find him. The journey cannot be made by car. We hire a two-passenger moto whose driver knows the twisted trails of the outback, and we ride off into the night.

—

In the middle of nowhere, my companion tells the driver to stop. Outside of the moto's little beam of light, all is black except for the moonless sea of stars overhead. My companion walks away, vanishing into the blackness, and a few minutes later returns. He tells me that he will lead me to his friend, then return to town. His friend will drive me back later.

His friend's hut stands high on stilts amid the boughs and rustling branches of trees. At the top of a bamboo ladder, the friend stands smiling. My companion says some words to him, and the friend welcomes me naturally and warmly as my companion leaves us.

The friend is younger than I, and he seems to

be a very happy man. He is lean, sinewy, and moves with slow grace. The walls of the hut are made of bamboo and woven strips of frond, its floor of slats. There is light from a small oil lamp, and from candles. His eyes are glassy. He has been smoking ganja from a water pipe, and he continues to do so as I sit on one of the hut's two soft and timeworn mats. That he knows I cannot understand him does not keep him from speaking to me, ever smiling, occasionally nodding in delight as if I have enjoyed or agreed with this or that observation of his.

Done with his ganja, he turns his attention to a chipped and cracked lacquer box, from which he takes a large soft black square that is wrapped in cellophane imprinted with little yellow pagodas. He unwraps the opium, places it on a lacquer tray that holds two small, sharp knives, a pair of thin-bladed scissors, a box of matches, a spindle fashioned from a bicycle spoke, a short rectangular strip of stiff dry frond, and an unlighted coconut-oil lamp whose glass chimney has been crafted by expertly cutting the bottom from a jelly-jar glass. Lifting a slat from the floor, he withdraws a cloth-wrapped opium pipe from a hidden compartment. The pipe is about eighteen inches long, made of dark carved wood, with a damper saddle of brass and a bowl of stone.

With one of the knives, he cuts off a piece of the opium, kneads and flattens it, and divides it into several equal parts. With the scissors, he trims the wick of the lamp. He strikes a match and lights the lamp, adjusting its homely chimney. The sweet, subtle scent of the oil laces the air. With the point of the spindle he takes a tiny piece of opium, places it on the piece of dry frond, and, over the chimneyed flame of the lamp, turns and rolls the opium with the spindle point until it is transformed into a perfect minuscule cone the consistency of soft, almost melted caramel, and the rich, tawny color of hazelnut.

He transfers this lovely morsel from the spindle point to the small hole at the center of the pipe's solid stone piece. As he reclines, mouth to pipe, he tilts the bowl over the lamp's chimney, holding it in place precisely where the alchemy can be wrought – the elusive 'sweet spot' – and sucks mightily. The opium bubbles, and the delicious perfume of the stuff, more beautiful than that of any garden, flowers unseeable and unknowable, mingles with color turned to scent, hue of tawny hazelnut to aroma of hazelnut roasting, foreshadowing more sublime synesthesia to come. Tending all the while with spindle point the bubbling opium in its tiny hole, he sucks until his cheeks are all high bone and taut concave flesh, an intense facial exercise that after some years leaves the imprint of the habit on the contours of the smoker's face: those 'Ho Chi Minh cheekbones,' by which every habituated smoker can recognize another.

———

The morsel done, he scrapes out the toxic residue from the damper, prepares another morsel, sets it in the pipe, and passes the sucking end to me, instructing me gently with words I do not comprehend as he positions, adjusts, and holds the pipe for me over the sweet spot of the lamp. My pattern of breath is wrong, and the bubbling opium extinguishes again and again. Finally, yes – he nods, there is the baptism of approval in his eyes – I have it: the vapors deep in my lungs, wisping full from the fastness of my mouth, the opium bubbling in luscious magic in the pipe bowl over the lamp. Then it is gone. There follows another pipeful for me, then one for him; yet another for me, another for him. We smile to each other from our parallel mats, the pipe and tray of implements between us. I offer him an American cigarette, which he takes with de-light. We lie back and smoke; and now, wordlessly, we understand each other perfectly in the eloquence of a silence that not only contains all that has ever been and all that ever will be said, but also drosses the vast babel of it, leaving only the ethereal purity of that wordless poetry that only the greatest of poets have glimpsed in epiphany. Their epiphanies seem to be borne for me to read in the cigarette smoke that swirls above me. Shakespeare – 'O learn to read what silent love hath writ' – entwined with Pound's great and final testament: 'I have tried to write Paradise / Do not move / Let the wind speak / that is paradise.'

To learn to read what silent love hath writ, to bow to the power of the wind. This is to live. This is to know that what one can say or write is as nothing before that silence and that power. The Ch'an master Niu-t'ou Fa-Yung, more than 1,300 years ago: 'How can we obtain truth through words?'

All that in the swirling smoke of a Marlboro Light.

Through rifts in the thatched roof, I can see the stars in the black of night. There are the sounds of night birds, the lone distant howls of creatures. Feral dogs? Wolves? Demons? No matter: those that fly and those that prowl, we are beneath the same stars, fleeting spirits born of and destined to the same almighty silence. The oldest word in Western literature, the word with which the *Iliad* began: rage. Yes. To speak is to rage against that silence whose winds are the only true poets. I think of Homer beholding these same stars. To rage, to kneel in wisdom before wisdom that is beyond wisdom. What does it matter? I grind out my cigarette. Another pipe for me, another for him. Another for me, another for him.

I am not going to rhapsodize here about opium. But I will say this: it is the perfect drug. There is nothing else like it. In this age of pharmaceutical-pill pushing, it delivers all that drugs such as Prozac promise. Forget about the medieval-like bugaboo of serotonin, the atrocities of Freud, the iatrogenic 'disorders' that compose the *Malleus Maleficarum* by which to-day's shrinks and psychopharmacologists con their vulnerable marks. All the pills and all the whoredom of psychotherapy in the world are nothing compared with the ancient Coptic words of the Gospel of Thomas: 'If you bring forth what is within you, what you bring forth will save you. If you do not bring forth what is within you, what you do not bring forth will destroy you.' It is as simple and unsolvable as that. Forget about the interplay of opium and serotonin. Its interplay with the wisdom of the Gospel of Thomas is the thing. Its vapors are of that thing within.

I believe that this is why this most delicately exquisite of intoxicants, this least stupefying of drugs – less so even than marijuana – is nevertheless so addictive. How could the taste of paradise be otherwise? Yes, of course, so much better it would be to possess that taste purely through understanding and living. But as wretched a thing as terminal opium addiction might be, it is no more wretched than addictions of more familiar and acceptable sorts.

Opium addicts can live to fine old ages, and can an addiction to paradise, artificial as it may be, be considered more ignoble than an addiction to television, movies, or the other lower artificialities of a world so vacant as to be aware of and conversant in the pseudoscience of serotonin but not of or in the wisdom of Thomas, a world so vacant as to be enamored of the false connoisseurship of rancid grape juice but not the true connoisseurship of something such as opium, let alone of life?

Enough of this profundity. The labor involved in its elucidation is far too great. You want enlightenment? Go get it yourself. Anyway, as I said – or was it one of those other guys? – paradise has no words.

———

And my friend in the hut, it turns out, has no moto. He has to walk a mile through the scrub to borrow a neighbor's. He does this. Before returning me to town, he rolls a cigarillo of ganja, mixing the ganja with the accumulated toxic residues of the opium pipe, and for good measure sprinkling it with a white crystalline powder that I take to be methedrine – *ya ba*, the new plague. I lie there watching him smoke it. When he is done, he stands, and we descend the bamboo ladder to an old and battered moto. We bolt off into the black of night, swerving at breakneck speed down unseen trails. He seems to know the place of every sharp bend, every furrow, and every rock, even though he cannot see them. I sit clutching the seat behind him. I can only wonder at the effects of his cigarillo. We begin to bounce roughly over big exposed roots of trees, splash whirring through splattering mud, branches and brush scraping now at an elbow or an ankle, then across the face. Turning to me with a laugh, he yells one of the few English words he knows: 'Shortcut.'

After one last high bouncing jolt over God knows what, we come down on a paved road. Now I can smell the moto's speed, and my friend's laughing, talking, and turned-away driving increase. The road is deserted, but the lights of Phnom Penh can be seen. It is maybe three or four in the morning. We zoom round a bend, the road widens, and there, before us, the police have set up a random checkpoint blockade. My friend slows as we near the police. They are still a good distance away, but they can discern our slowing down, and they relax their stance and lower their machine guns. It is then that my friend, turning to me with renewed and invigorated laughter, pats the tank of the moto as if it were the flank of a horse, then jolts dead straight ahead at full speed through the blockade, never turning to look, but jabbering and laughing to me all the while. We are past the blockade, still moving at full speed – faster now, suddenly downhill, when the machine-gun fire is heard like long strips of firecrackers going off behind us. Are they shooting at us or over us? My friend swerves off the road, onto another, then another, emerges at a bridge, beyond which he swerves again, and there, as if from nowhere, is the entrance to my hotel. He wishes me a fond farewell, and he is off again into the night.

—

I learn in Phnom Penh that there is but one opium boatman left of the many who once plied the turbulent Mekong. He is an old man, and after him, the river trade will end. Every month, he comes downriver, stopping at a few ports – Phnom Penh is one of them – where he sells opium to individual smokers and to those who deal in pellets for eating. In these same ports, he buys or barters for cheap clothing, which he brings back upriver to sell. His home port is unknown, but his monthly journey downriver is believed to begin near the heart of the Golden Triangle.

This phrase, which bears an air of Oriental ancientry, is really rather recent in origin, and gained currency, after the French *Triangle d'Or*, during the 1960s, when the war in Vietnam produced the biggest heroin boom in history, leading to the making of innumerable new fortunes from the region's poppy fields. It is precisely defined by the three points where Thailand, Myanmar, and Laos near one another, at the confluence of the Mekong and Ruak Rivers: Sop Ruak in northern Thailand, the Shan-country headland southwest of Tachilek in Myanmar, and the western headland of Bokeo Province in Laos. The Golden Triangle, in its extended sense, encompasses more than 86,000 square miles of territory, the poppy-growing heart of Asia, and the heart, too, of the entwined violent serpents of tribal insurrections and the drug trade.

In Sop Ruak, the defining Thai point of the Golden Triangle, one encounters the House of Opium: a modest museum with historical displays, antique pipes, and rusted artifacts. This seems to confirm my worst fears, for when anything is deemed museum-worthy, then surely it is dead. Without walking too far, one may look across the Mekong to the lawless Shan lands of Myanmar.

And what might that structure on the other side be? Nothing less than the construction site of the Golden Triangle Paradise Resort.

I sit in the breakfast room of the hotel in Chiang Mai, a hundred or so miles south. Another morning, another cup of coffee, another cigarette. Almost everybody I've met who has visited northern Thailand has encountered a tribal villager eager to administer a pipe or two of opium for cash. Invariably, those who have smoked it have gotten sick and little else from it. I have before me a business card of a trekking outfit. These are the people who take you to the villages of the tribes where you smoke the opium that makes you sick. I want to be back in the wild country outside Phnom Penh, lying in that hut amid the trees, looking at the stars through the shivering rifts in the thatch.

Another cup of coffee, another cigarette. I have never read a Graham Greene tale in my life, but suddenly I find I have entered a passage from one.

'Did they tell you in Bangkok that I was looking forward to meeting you?'

They? Who were they? I look up at a well-dressed, pleasant-seeming man whose English is so blithely enunciated that one never would think that it is to him the second of several languages.

'No,' I say.

He asks politely if he might join me for a moment. He speaks circuitously awhile, as propriety might behoove, leading me to the place where I, not he, openly state, as propriety does indeed behoove, the nature of my quest. He knows the politics of the drug trade well. I ask him if much has changed since the retirement a few years ago of the Shan leader Khun Sa, the infamous 'prince of death,' who was believed to be the most powerful of the Golden Triangle's drug lords.

'Not really, except perhaps for the loss of a colorful bit of local legendry.'

Odd, I say, as I had long believed him to be the true potentate of the heroin trade.

'Certainly most would have been led to believe so. But I think perhaps the true power lay elsewhere.' For a fleeting moment, I have the strange notion that he is speaking of himself.

He rises, tidies himself, smiles pleasantly. 'Anyway, I have a friend who may be able to help you. I'll give him a ring, and, if it's convenient for you, I'll meet you back here at eleven.'

Then he is gone.

⁓

His friend accommodates us with an ashtray, perhaps as we have been gracious enough to remove our shoes without prompting before entering his Buddhist home. All I know of him is what the Graham Greene character has told me during our drive here to his home in the quiet countryside outside Chiang Mai: that he is a scholar and an opium master, fluent both in English and Chinese, and that he is a Buddhist, which means that I should remove my shoes at his threshold.

'Yeah,' he is saying, 'I've seen the way those tribal guys prepare their opium. They boil it, run it through dirty socks, add a lot of dross, a lot of toxic pipe-head residue. I've seen them mix in these big yellow pills, morphine or whatever. To their way of thinking, it goes further that way. But they're not smoking opium. They're smoking shit. Most people in this world who think they've smoked opium have only smoked shit.'

Connoisseurs, he says, argue as to the source of the finest opium. Some say the best opium comes from Patna, India, along the southern bank of the Ganges. Others believe that the best opium is cultivated in the Lao sector of the Golden Triangle.

The processing of the opium into paste for smoking, however, is more important than the opium itself. *Yen-gao*, this smoking-paste is called in Chinese; *chandoo*, in India and South-east Asia.

Besides contamination by the blending in of

the toxic pipe-head scrapings, raw opium is subject to the addition of all sorts of noxious substances to increase its weight for sale, from gum arabic to molasses to tree mastics. The first step in the purification process is to submerge a loaf of raw opium, usually a brick of from one to two kilograms, overnight in a large pot of clear springwater. The next day, the pot should be brought to a full boil and whisked thoroughly for fifteen minutes to completely dissolve the raw opium. As all of the many active opium alkaloids are fully water-soluble, this process separates the active opium essence from the inert vegetable matter. The pot is then removed from the heat and set to rest until the inert matter settles to a sediment. The contents of the pot are then filtered through a sieve lined with finely woven cotton or silk. The filtered sediment then undergoes a secondary boiling, whisking, and filtering. The two filtered liquids are then combined and filtered yet again, with whatever sediment collects being discarded.

The liquid is then set aside in a large covered vessel for two days. Further filterings, further sedimentations follow. After ten days or so, a final boiling, simmering, and reduction is completed. Further steps involve the addition of a cup of good brandy, to kill any spores that may have grown during sedimentation, and to help blend, balance, and enrich the active alkaloids. The brandy is added as the opium brew simmers, thus evaporating the alcohol and not degrading the smoking paste.

—

In the end a two-kilo loaf of raw opium yields perhaps one kilo of purest *chandoo*, which then may be consumed forthwith or set to age for years in porcelain or other ceramic jars sealed with cork and beeswax.

'Have fifteen-year-old. Have thirteen-year-old, have twelve-year-old. What you want?'

Aged opium?

Yes, aged opium. There are reputed yet to be, in the dark, cool cloisters of the wealthiest connoisseurs, fine porcelain urns of opium, subtly and elegantly fermenting, now for eighty years and more, from the exclusive special stocks of the grandest of the old Shanghai salons.

Among those connoisseurs is one of the most celebrated fashion designers in Paris, reputed to possess the greatest collection of opium pipes in the world. (A collection of fine, vintage opium pipes would include imperial specimens of carved ivory and gold, white jade, and rare shagreen; pipes of three hundred years' age and more.) The designer is an importer of purest *chandoo*. What costs the equivalent of $500 in Laos – enough *chandoo* to last an addict for a year: 450 grams – costs twice that in Chiang Mai. By the time it reaches Paris, its price per gram is precisely that of gold on the day of its arrival.

While the purification of raw opium into *chandoo* lies at the heart of the opium master's art, there are other matters attendant to his supervision of the smoking itself. The choice of oil; the amount of oil to be placed in the lamp well; the materials and construction of the lamp (*yen-tene*); the spindle, scraper, and more: these are all concerns to be reckoned with. Our host, who prefers oil of coconut because of its delicacy and faintness of scent as well as the temperature coefficient of the heat generated by its burning, tells of an old Chinese preference for rendered pig fat. Concerning the pipe itself – *yen-tsiang*, 'the smoking gun' – our host is a traditionalist who abides by the simple perfection of seasoned bamboo, a saddle of silver, a bowl of kiln-dried red terra-cotta. Opium, if it is to be kept on hand for ready use, should be stored in a container of silver. These are, he assures me, but the rudiments of an ancient, arcane, and closed knowledge. He tells me of a volume, which he believes will soon be published, that promises to reveal this knowledge in full and in the context of the lore and true history of opium. (I have since glimpsed – and blurbed – this book, *The Big Smoke: The Chinese Art & Craft of Opium*, by Peter Lee, and I can say that it seems to be a work of astonishing breadth and depth, and by far the most valuable treatise on opium that we are likely ever to have. Published in Thailand by Lamplight Books, Ltd., as this piece was being prepared for press, *The Big Smoke* has not yet found an American or British publisher brave enough to take it on, and so, at least for now, the book remains highly elusive outside of Asia. The interested reader is referred to: http://taolodge.com.tw/bigsmoke.)

'Shall we have some, then?' our host asks.

We adjourn to a room of cushions and pillows and many books, and the equipment he has so knowingly described, from the terra-cotta-bowled pipe of aged bamboo to the lamp and spindle to the little silver canister full of purest *chandoo*.

The wick is trimmed, the lamp lit. Our host dips his bodkin into the canister, rolls and kneads the *chandoo* on the flat surface of the pipe's bowl, held aslant above the heat of the lamp.

'The idea,' he says, 'is to soften it, not burn it.' Slowly, as he works it, the dark *chandoo* turns a creamy golden brown. He centers the damper over the flame, to heat its tiny hole, then inserts the soft golden *chandoo* with the point of the bodkin so as to leave a pinhole at its center.

He extends the mouthpiece to me, tends to the position of the pipe and the steady coddling of the bubbling *chandoo*. The taste, the scent – yes, there is to them that lovely, sweet-roasting hazelnut aroma, that delicate perfume of unknown flowers; but these are just the airs that drift through what can only be called ambrosia. My lungs cannot have enough of it, so unimaginable the taste, so soft and gentle the vapors.

'If you bring forth what is within you, what you bring forth will save you. If you do not bring forth what is within you, what you do not bring forth will destroy you.'

I am aswirl, bird-soul and breeze, amid the cool high mountain trees of the myriad-meaninged knowledge of that thing, savior and destroyer, within. Never has an afternoon passed in such serenity, in life lived so fully, so freely of the maggots of that glob of gross crenulated meat that we call mind. To be here now, wordless, every breath a bringing forth, peering calm and adrift through the interstices of forever.

Back in the other room, our host sits with a sketch pad on his knees, bowed over it, pencil in hand. He sits upright, tears the topmost sheet from the pad, and extends it to me.

'Here. This should help you find it.'

He then hands me a big vacuum-packed bag of tea. 'The old man's name is Chiang. Give him this from me.'

Somewhere in Indochina, in a crumbling city whose streets have no names, I walk out into the noonday heat and dust, unfold the hand-drawn street map, and gather my bearings. Nothing has ever seemed so simple: the fountain at one end of town, the temple at the other, and a road leading from the temple to a Honda shop, near where, on a backstreet, up the rickety stairs of a shack on stilts, I will find what I have sought.

Hours later, in the increasing heat and dust, I find myself still wandering, looking at the homely map again and again, clutching the bag of tea beneath my arm. While there are few other signs of commerce, there are at least three Honda shops, and every backstreet is crowded with nothing but old wooden shacks on stilts. Occasionally, when it seems to be the shack indicated on the map, as viewed from this perspective, then that, I call to a shack's open door or paneless window: 'Chiang *ici?*'

I wander on amid beggars and goats and dogs and chickens nesting in roadside garbage. This dying city is the dross of a former French colonial outpost now being reclaimed by the jungle and by dirt and dust where paved roads had been. But no one seems to understand my pidgin French, or to recognize the name of Chiang.

Night falls. After dinner at a Chinese restaurant, I meander to the fountain at the end of town. There are colored lanterns strung, signs of life, plastic tables and chairs, grim-looking girls serving coffee and drinks. In this city that shuts at midnight, all will soon be dark and silent here.

It is a city of many snakes. The night is diffused only by the dim soft glowings of the colored lantern lights. From the corner of my eye, I see a huge slithering creature moving nearby: a python of great and frightening girth. But its upraised eyes behold my own, and its eyes are human: a beggar with no limbs writhing sinuously among the tables on the dark cool earth. His human eyes turn cold, like those of a naga. Perhaps he is not a beggar at all. Perhaps he is merely of this place.

———

The next morning, on a street which does indeed have a name, I approach a clutch of loitering drivers amid their samlors and tuk-tuks on a corner where a big wooden building leans precipitously. I show them my map, with its landmarks. The men crowd round it gibbering, grabbing it back and forth. Sounds of recognition are followed by sounds of dismissal. After much debate among themselves and haphazard pointing in this direction and that, one of them snatches the map from another, folds it, returns it to me, climbs into his tuk-tuk, starts the motor, and, with no indication, waits for me to clamber aboard. The vehicle sputters around the corner, rattles several yards through patches of parched earth and mud, then comes to an idling halt before what, set back from the road a bit, is yet another shack on stilts.

I approach the regulation rickety slat stairs, ascend one step, and I can smell it: the most lovely smell on earth. At the top of the rickety stairs is a rickety door. Above the door is nailed a piece of wood painted with the image of a protective spirit-creature, sword in mouth, beneath the octagonal symbol of the Chinese

Eight Trigrams. I knock, then knock again. The head and shirtless upper body of a young man protrude from the window to my left, waving me in.

I enter a dark room at the far side of which is an altar in shambles. The shirtless young man appears, beckons me up a step into another room. There, on the floor, are the bamboo mats, the trays of lamps, pipes, and other implements. A few men recline on their sides, their heads resting on little wooden pillow-benches.

'Chiang *ici*?'

'Papa, *oui*,' the young man responds. He leaves the room through a second doorway, which leads to a sagging porch of sorts. He returns with an old man shuffling in tow.

'Chiang?'

The old man nods. I present him with the bag of tea. He beams, beholds it as if it were treasure. He gently kicks one of the supine men, rousing him, summoning him to rise, then gestures that I take his place on the mat.

Another man appears, shirtless, shoeless, hunkering on the other side of the tray that lies by my head. He, too, though quite a bit older than the man who led me in, refers to Chiang as Papa. Soon I will learn that it is not a matter of bloodline. It is what one properly calls the lord of the den: Papa.

As I lie there, looking about, I recall my old romantic visions of the opium den where I was born to lie: the dark brocade curtains and velvet cushions of luxurious decadence, the lovely loosened limbs of recumbent exotic concubines. Well, Chiang's old lady may have loose limbs, but those are the only adjective and the only noun of my visions that here pertain. The place really is a dive.

It is then that I recall every reliable account of an opium den that I have read or heard. Except for the golden-era salons of Shanghai, public opium dens had always been dives. From the first New York City newspaper account of an opium den of 131 years ago – the same year,

1869, that Charles Dickens's visits to the opium dens of Ratcliffe Highway, London, elicited similar descriptions – to the account, eighty-five years later, of the last opium den in New York, that is how they had all been depicted: as dives. Where had I gotten those fucking brocade curtains from?

Chiang tells the pipe man that there is to be no charge – I learn this later – and that I am to be invited to share in any meal. He himself prepares for me a little pot of good black tea to sip between pipes. It is as if money, even in this poorest of places, no longer has anything to do with any of it: not with him, not with the opium, not with this place. It is as if he, like the old image above the door, is here now only to do what he was born to do, and to ward off the end of a dying world of which he alone remains.

The lamp is lit, the pipe is tilted. I am home.

A NOTE ON THE AUTHOR

Born in Newark and schooled in his father's bar, Nick Tosches is the author of acclaimed biographies of Dean Martin (*Dino*), the Mafia financier Michele Sindona (*Power on Earth*), Sonny Liston (*The Devil and Sonny Liston*), and Jerry Lee Lewis (*Hellfire*); of two books about popular music (*Country* and *Unsung Heroes of Rock 'n' Roll*); and of the novels *Trinities* and *Cut Numbers*. His most recent book is *Where Dead Voices Gather*. His is a contributing editor at *Vanity Fair*.

A NOTE ON THE TYPE

The text of this book is set in Bembo. This type
was first used in 1495 by the Venetian printer
Aldus Manutius for Cardinal Bembo's *De Aetna*,
and was cut for Manutius by Francesco Griffo.
It was one of the types used by Claude Garamond
(1480–1561) as a model for his Romain
de L'Université, and so it was the forerunner
of what became standard European type for
the following two centuries. Its modern form
follows the original types and was designed
for Monotype in 1929.